In the Absence of My Father

By Lena M. Fields-Arnold

Emperor Publishing
Dayton, OH

Copyright © 2009

Lena M. Fields-Arnold

All Rights Reserved.
No Part of this book may be reproduced or transmitted in any form or by any means, electrical or mechanical, including photocopying and recording, or by any information storage or retrieval systems except as may be expressly permitted by the Copyright Act or in writing from the author/publisher.

ISBN: 978-0-9795613-4-4
Library of Congress Control Number: 2009937385

Published by Emperor Publishing
Cover conversion and layout — JUST INK Digital Design
Printed in the USA

Buried Inside

In the Absence of my Father	6
Dear Coach	8
Destined	10
Michael	11
Funeral Scene	12
Someone Father Me	17
Child Molester	18
Just Wondering	20
Who Decided	21
Separation Scene	22
End of the dance	23
Sonnet in September	24
Sweet Surrender	25
A Mother's Observation	26
Let Me See What You Look Like	27
Through My Father's Eyes	28
The Report Card	29
The Kiss Off	30
For My Fathers	31
Family Reunion	36
Father and Son	38

The Legacy of You	40
Mold	42
The Bird's Nest	43
Daddy Daddy	45
The Park	48
Death of an Empire	49
Love Scene	50
Memories of You	52
On the Cusp of Age 11	53
On Sunday	58
What I Heard Was	60
The Good Father	61
On Stone Ground	63
No More Excuses	64
Forgiveness Haiku	65
father	66
Father	67
The Finish	68

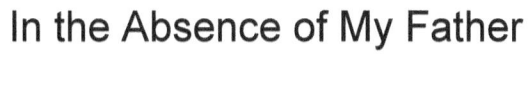

In the Absence of my Father

In the absence of my father,
    I became someone I hate.
In the absence of my father,
    I steered 'way from positive fate.

In the absence of my father,
    I listened to deceitful voices.
In the absence of my father,
    I made all the wrong choices.

In the absence of that guided hand,
    in the absence of words of praise;
I wandered through foreign lands,
    and fell ill to myriad malaise.

In the absence of my father I lost my way,
    'though hard my mother prayed.
In the absence of my father,
    my maturity was delayed.

In the absence of my father,
    I became a stagnant player.
In the absence of his calming voice,
    I evolved into a depressing naysayer.

In the absence of someone to believe in,
    evil works seeped into my brain.
In the absence of my father,
    I could not erase their malevolent stain.

In The Absence of My Father

In the absence of my father's
    optimistic words of affirmation;
I lived in a constant state
    of self-hate and degradation.

In the absence of my father,
    life was difficult because;
In the absence of my father,
    I never learned to truly love.

Dear Coach:

This letter is to respectfully inform you
that I am quitting the team.
I'm tired of sitting on the bench
as towel boy for the second string.
I know how to play the game.
I'm a strong team player.
I can give you my undivided attention
And in case I failed to mention
My unconditional love too.
Well, I could have.
You refused to let me stay in the game;
preferring to play the weak, immature and needy.
What's that about coach?

So I just wanted you to know
that I am walking away.
I don't know what more I can say!
I was the first one on the squad–
first one to line-up at practice.
I tried to talk to you about this before,
-you just kept shutting the door.
You say you love me too.
I don't see it.
Spending all your free time
with the pathetic, scrawny, and weedy.
Then you want me to train them as well?

So I'm getting out of the game.
Don't know if I will ever play again.
Here's my uniform.
Don't want to be part of a group
where I never win.
Even a loser needs
a victory now and then.

destined

you gonna miss it
if you walk out on me 'cause
what i'm gonna be

is preordained from above
destined to achieve great things

Michael

he's a grown man
yet he still cannot eject the negative tape
out of his head
something keeps compelling him to push play

he's an adult
yet he still lives in a world
of derogatory thought
no matter
how many positive things to him i say

content to forever
play the part of victim
he feigns the role of warrior
fighting in a world
of self-imposed addiction
enveloping himself
in its faux, protective barrier

what did your father do
to you what cruel words were spoken
that i now find myself
trying to heal your wounds
and attempting to repair
a psyche that has been broken

i alone am witness
to damage that cannot be undone
when a father destroys his own son

Funeral Scene

I mourn today
for what I don't remember.
For a happiness that I have to reach
way back into at least 33 years ago to find.
I lament
that I am forced to rummage around
in the attic of my mind;
and hunt for memories of goodness
so old that I must
wipe the dust off of them.

There I will find recollections
of a father who cared.
The high priest of our home
who made time for us.
Who found pleasure in our laughter.
So much so
that he
played games with us,
carted us
to the amusement park
to the beach,
to all manner of destinations of fun.

I will remember a daddy
who carefully strung up Christmas lights
to light up for us the dark holiday nights.
who surreptitiously
eavesdropped in on our
Christmas wishes.

In The Absence of My Father

who filled our lives
with Valentines Day Kisses.
bid us good Easter desires and
who pulled our feet
from the destroyers fires.

In that upper floor I will uncover memoirs
of happier moments spent
watching the cars race around with him;
and learning to ride my bike with him;
being spun around till I was dizzy by him.

I bemoan the fact that now
I have to scratch the surface of my pate
Just to relate
to what should be a day of physical grief.
Instead I grieve for me!
I grieve for what I know can never, ever, ever again be!
A father who cared about me!

Because now my grief is clouded
by the little moments of uncertainty;
fogged up by the instances when
I didn't know for sure if he cared to see
all the tears I shed over what used to be!

I'm trying so hard not to unearth the dirt
in this here garret
because if I poke around too long up here
I will also find the things
I have struggled too long to forget.

Like the first time my high priest
slipped from his precipice;
lost his formal place of worship in my spirit.
The moment when my father went
from being the one I trusted to protect me;
to being the one I feared would hurt me.
I remember now,
it was the first time I saw him hit my mother.

That was the real moment my father died for me!

Over the years he would die a little more in my heart.
With each strike of his fist into her tear filled face
He would die again!
With each rape-
with each anguished cry in the night!
He passed on into the abyss and right out of my heart.
With every night spent away from home
Was a night he was misplaced by my heart.
With each indiscretion and each extra-marital affair
he expired anew.
With each infant borne
by the mistress
I mourned!
With every step child he supported instead of me.
I grieved because time spent with them
was time lost with me.
Competing against lesser opponents
Who shouldn't even be in the game?
They don't even bear your last name.
And when I tried to make you understand-make you see-
Then you threatened to hit me!
The baby girl you once lovingly
Bounced on your knee

In The Absence of My Father

You were going to hit me?
And I am still grieving
And nobody sees my tears
Nobody cared about them then
And I wish I didn't care now.
See because
Today is my second funeral.
Today marks the second time I have wept
for what will by no means ever be.
A daughter
who was once told that **she**
was the apple of her fathers eye;
should never have to cry
over vanished days gone by.
And I
Oh, yes I still cry.
Because I remember the good times
and I remember the bad times
And those times are all muddled together
like a little child's painting.
You know-how they start out with the bright colors,
but because they don't know what they are doing
they begin adding too much paint
until the picture is one big glop of boo boo brown.

And what started out with promise
is a picture you can't fix;
and that cute little child looks at it
and thinks they have created a masterpiece.
Too ignorant to know that they have just destroyed
something
that had the potential to be beautiful.

This is the funeral procession I ride in.
The limo of this funeral
consigns me to precarious destinations.
And I weep sorely
because I don't want to go there.

Someone Father Me

Silent——the sound of pen on paper. Free?
Wondering when will someone father me?

So I signed the contract, left the press and
shuffled out crying someone father me.

I screamed, inside my head nerve endings ripe!
Now I need to call someone, father me!

Shouting at him through lines, "Can we be we?"
Please man I needed someone Father. Me

I hold the drink up. Toast to being free.
Lena Arnold needs someone. Father? Me!

Child Molester

Who invited this stranger in
to steal my childhood again and again?
His dark shadows fill my head
with evil, tormenting, thoughts of dread.

Who can I tell of the pain and fear?
If I shout will anyone hear?
Who gave him the right to enter my place?
Who decided he could violate my space?

I want to scream, but I am afraid to cry!
His power overwhelms me and I'm afraid I'll die!
Tell me, who invited this stranger in
who comes to me in the guise of friend?

He smiles but 'neath his murderous grin,
Is the smile of an enemy, not that of a friend.
Mommy, mommy, do you not see?
Why won't you end what he is doing to me?

Don't you hear him when he leaves your bed?
Can't you see when he's near I am filled with dread?
If I tell you, who will you blame?
With whom can I share my secret shame?

Tell me mommy, who invited him in?
Will you please put him out so he can't hurt me again?
Does anyone observe how I cringe when he's around;
see my pain, or notice my head's always down?

In The Absence of My Father

Don't you notice my nervous clinging to you?
When I feebly smile it's a sham I hope you see through.
Are you even aware that my grades dropped,
and I've cut my hair?
Do you ever notice the blood in my underwear?

Can't you spot the dark shadows underneath my eyes?
Hear in the night my muffled, anguished cries?
Tell me please, **who invited** this stranger in,
to steal my childhood again and again?

Just wondering

I wonder if you
would cry with me or
care to know that I
was molested 'cause
you abdicated
responsibility
failed to monitor
your investment see
was just wondering?

Who Decided

Who decided that I didn't need you?
    Whose voice convinced you
        that you were unimportant to me?

To whose words did you listen
    when you decided to leave?
    Who told you that I would not grieve?

Who said your kisses were irrelevant?
    Who influenced you not
        to chase away my monsters at night?

Whose words did convey to you
    this horrible lie?
Who is this false informant
    who said I wouldn't cry?

Separation Scene

She
Feels justified
To creep at night
'cause she crying
And she up tight

He
Feels justified
To be reckless
Think nothing wrong
Being selfish

She
In the middle
Of something she
Don't understand
She
Thinks it's her fault
Her momma can't
Keep her own man

He
In the middle
Of something he
Will never know
He
Think he why his
Daddy never
Come home no more

End of the dance

i never expected you to be perfect
i did however expect you to be there
i never expected you to be free of sin
i did however expect that you'd care

daddy
this dance is getting old
it's time to stop the music
the record has been distorted
and scratched for a long time
it's broken
and
i'm tired of this tango
the salsa has no spice
the many dances long lost their momentum
no jazz
no zing
no dynamism
so let's end it here
me at thirty-nine
you at sixty-one
i will call it-dance over
relationship-done

Sonnet in September

She dance on wind high, taught by her father.
Come calls her mother, day now drawing nigh.
Off porch steps daughter, dance slower with sigh.
"Ah, no crying girl," says he to daughter.
In arms up she climbs, he sings lullaby.
Quiets her with, "Hush now – kiss moon goodbye."
Teach her to dance she asks why he bothers.
"Bother 'cause I love you girl child of night.
So dance on in dream sleep and remember.
This dance I teach now be your strength to fight."
Be witness to me moon in September.
That I taught the dance to her true and right.
So she stays pure when comes her December.

Sweet Surrender

Sleepy heads rest on
bosom of their papa; wait
on rest patiently.

This is gift that father gives.
Means safety net from bad dreams.

A Mother's Observation

Bold boys brave bubbles.
Splash on Splash water cloud up-
planes down crash landing!

Papi fights hard laugh.
Insides roll and toss glee; whale
rolls in, eats planes up.

Bravely boys bubble
beat while Papi's whale swim 'way,
through a bubble sea.

Let Me See What You Look Like

Say you love me
Be lovely to me as flowers to grass
Give way to my heart as lads to lass
And let me see what you look like
When the dawn breaks

Say you adore me
Be sweet to me as moon is to sky
Fancy me as love birds on high
And let me see what love looks like
When I awake

Say you love me
Be to my spirit as candy to lips
Yield to my heart as kindness to kiss
And let me see what you look like
Casting lines into lake

Say you adore me
Be charming to me as princes in tales
Hide not from me as princesses veiled
And let me see what love looks like
In the mirror of face

Let me feel what love feels like
In the hug of your hand
Let me hear what love sounds like
In the accent of a man
Say you love me
And that you'll show me what you look like

Through My Father's Eyes

My purity was never compromised.
I never opened up my womanhood
nor yielded my fruits to men I despised.
I never fell prey to men of no good.
Neither did I believe their twisted lies.
Because I got to see how men could be;
through my caring, and loving father's eyes.
They never had the chance to prey on me.
Your eyes were lights that lead me to the Lord;
kept my feet on the best paths to pursue.
Safely led me to the near proper shore—
eternal summer always bright and true.
From you father I gained the strength to stand;
guided by your faithful, firm, loving hand.

3rd Grade Report Card

Reading	A+
Math	A
Language	A+
Art	B
Gym	A
Social Studies	A
Science	A

Teacher's Comments:

Changes in Lena I notice,
starkly different from when in first grade.
She seems to be easily agitated,
though her academics have not been delayed.
No one can say anything to her,
for she takes it all personally.
If one says a word out of order,
she kicks that poor kid in the knee!
Seems she is always ready to fight.
Is everything alright?
Is little Lena okay?
I just wanted to know,
where is the sweet Lena of first grade?

The Kiss Off

winter cast its chill
upon our relationship
cold winds blow through bones

exposed as leafless trees to
conserve life in barren times

iced unfertile ground
shielding heart from frost; patient-
ly waiting for spring

For my Fathers

I

to your daughter
what kind of father were you
were you kind to them as to me
kind as the day when the breeze is soft
as a puppy's fur
kind as the smell that amuses nostrils
and conveys bliss

II

did you father them as **Mr. Clancy**
who sat on his porch often
talking the talk of listening and love
to all the daughters of the street

> "hey gurl! Watchu doing walkin' wit' yo head down?
> "Hol' it up high! You ain't nobody's sheep dog
> "Boy, leave dat girl 'lone 'fo I pop u one!
> "she ain't no stinky frog.
> Dat gurl is a queen."

in those moments
we forgot all about our troubles.

III

did you father them as **Uncle Moe**

dreams stillborn in his youth
he had a hundred children
in the nieces and nephews
who loved him
in every backgammon/dominoes/ checkers/chess
game played
a new child was birthed in his too patient explanations of
repeated rules
embracing every repetitive question as a father hugs his
newborn

he loved us as the precious Morning Glories
he carefully cultivated in his backyard

IV

did you father them as **A.D. Jones**

who worked the works of love
steadfast through the adversity
hardship and tough times
a persevering lifeline
to daughters drowning
sheltering like the God he served
protector of helpless women
with the roots planted deeply south.

V

did you father them as **Uncle Scoots**

whose love was rowdy and mischievous
like strong drink
and too much wine
yet never misdirected
never malevolent

> "Marie, of all my nieces you are the prettiest.
> I sure do think you are the smartest one too!
> Don't tell the rest of them I said that though
> 'cause they might get jealous."

Then, with a wink and a smile he walked away;
asking for nothing in return and taking nothing.

bringing only words of affirmation
that birthed insulation
in pretty, unaware, prepubescent girls
and kept us
from falling prey to satanic seducers

VI

did you father them as **Uncle Bruce**

who though divorced
didn't use it as an excuse to abandon his family
demonstrating responsibility
above child support payments

in activities extra-curricular
even in support of children extra-testicular
    Probably even taught them how to make pizza too

VII

did you father them as **Jimmy**?

a toothless roaring lion
with tigers claws
treacherous as a tornado
if his loved ones are in harms way
but soft as summer rain
tender of heart
creating time for every game and for every recital
being what he always wanted
but didn't have

VIII

did you father them as **Mark**?

protector of the weak and abused
the Masters apprentice
working three jobs to take care of his wife and kids
and who still finds time
to repair a broken bicycle
salvage a rusty motorbike
and cook dinner
all in the same night

VIIII

did you father them as **my love**

who loves as God
perfect and without fear
moving heaven and earth to bear the fruit
earth would dare deny
holding creation accountable
keeping promises made to God
during night terrors

I will do your will
I will raise them to honor your name
I will cultivate seed in wind, in rain, in storm, in tumults
In calm, in sunshine, in contentment

X

did you father them as **God**

carefully creating them from dust of the earth
and breathing into them the breath of life
masterfully planting them in a garden
and cultivating it to be free of strife
loving them enough to give them free will
and even in disobedience, loves them still
breathing
living
crying
dying
love

Family Reunion

sitting here on benches of wood
i fancy myself as a piece of its work
cut into this rectangular shape
and forced ingloriously into this spot
fixed
forces beyond my control
shaping my destiny
telling me
this is where i must be
and i in silent wonderment
shout
why me?

looking upward from this spot
at body appendages
of all shapes and sizes
and in various stages of
growth,
   stink,
      dry rot
from which i cannot
turn away
   this curious historical perspective
where people
play

back   forth
     and
forth   back
     and
surface tensions

In The Absence of My Father

simmering passions
underlying anger
issues unexplored
fathers with multiple families
trying to make two
tables fit together
today
as on many days
these counters will not form
and I am forced to watch

Father and Son

i left the audience of the movie
boldly stepped out of my seat i did,
walked up to them.
trying my best not to sound
insulting
asked them straight out i did

> *are you his father*
> *is this your dad*

his strong dark hand
took hold its smaller likeness
in protectiveness held it
and as kite fell from sky
asked of me
> *why*

the illogical reasoning of my mind
nearly rendered me dumb
trying my best to mask my astonishment
finding no pretense for my shock
words spilled from my lips a tsunami
of preconceived notions and stereotypes
made real by the daily farce of
newscasts worldwide
how could i mask my shame as i said

> *i was told this doesn't happen here*
> *this happy scene of jovial, frivolity*
> *this carefree picture of joy and contentment*
> *this loving depiction of father and son*

In The Absence of My Father

waiting for an outburst of anger and
anticipating words from the usher
silencing my unexpected superficial ruminations
briefly i stood
as he said poetically

> *flowers bloom where they are planted*
> *popular opinion aside*
> *there are many flowers blossoming here*

then the wind of God lifted the kite
from its earthly prison
stirring me from my reverie

moving away from my intrusion
father and son rushed after it
as it desired to fly high
as dreams do desire
moving on to my destination
i stepped back into the role of spectator
forever changed
yearning to fly-free

The Legacy of You

You
Have shown us
That we are a people
Bonded
By the courage
Of our ancestors
You
Have shown us the way
Because of you
We are proud
And strong
And fearless
And wise
Because of you
We know that even when we fall
We can still rise
Because of you
We dream of better tomorrows
Bright futures and expected ends
You
Have shown us
Love
life
laughter
because of your tears
Wiped dry by your commitment to excellence
We know that we can live
dream big
Even after we make mistakes
Like if I confuse you
With a cousin

In The Absence of My Father

Or call you by your sister's name
Or God forbid, do far worse than that
Your legacy-well
It only serves as a reminder
That our lives are too busy
And that we need to fellowship more
Because You
Taught us that family matters
We have grown
Too far apart and it's time to close the ranks,
tighten the clan, strengthen, and
solidify the bonds
that have made us strong
Made us who we are
We are listening for your voice now
We have heard your call
To remember who we are
That we are from a people who stand
strong and tall
A people who shake off the dust and rise when they fall
From a clan who believes in hope
in dreams
A nation of people reaching up for the
brass ring
You have shown us all this and more
That
We were the blessings worth waiting for
We thank you now and honor your fight
For through your dark hours we have been blessed to
see the light
Surrounded now by your witness,
O' mighty kings and queens
We will continue to love, to live,
to hope, to plan, to dream.

Mold

Malleable is
the mind of a child. For shame
or for our honor.

Into which vessel will you
mold your loving child into?

The Birds Nest

Watching through window
silently
with great anger and,
before she could
stop him.
She saw him lift the baby bird from its nest.
Its mother
seeking sustenance
left it vulnerable.
Try as he might
he could not be gentle in his caress.
The little bird
slipped
      from
            his
                  hands
            hitting hard ground.

Crying
he placed
the bird back
nest.   in
    the

Too late—
damage done and
hoping
his mother hadn't seen.
"*Leave the nest alone. Birds are not toys.*
They are too fragile for your hands."
"*But my hands are small and soft.*

I will be gentle, I promise."
Now
his mother's words
came back to haunt him.
Suddenly!
A quick
Shocking
Minute of momentary enlightenment—
He understood his mother's tears
when she spoke of his father.
A man
he had never known.
A man
who like him
once disturbed a birds nest
much too soon.
Now watching through window
silently,
with great compassion and
before she could comfort him;
he placed his face in his hands
and began to cry.

In The Absence of My Father

Daddy! Daddy!
How come I only see you twice a year?
And when I do, there are 15 other kids here?
And they all got the same last name?
And like me, they wear the same mask of shame.
They mask it well,
Because that's what kids do.
But we all gonna grow up to hate you.
'Cause we never hardly spend
No time with you
So how can we really value-You?
But we gonna keep on
Smilin' at you.
Especially when
The child's supports due!
But we can never really love you.

And what do your initials stand for anyway?

Poo-tang diddler?
Mind fiddler?
Take your kids brain
And bend it like a twizzler?
Or maybe they just stand for part-time daddy

Daddy! Daddy!
I'm scared; can I sit on your lap?
Daddy! Daddy! I'm tired
will you put me down for a nap?
"Sorry baby, mommy don't know where daddy at!"
Are you in France daddy, parlay vous layin'?
I want to believe that you out somewhere prayin.
But you probably with some other chick sayin',

"Have my baby, baby, for real-I ain't playin'!"
Momma I don't understand
Why you made the decision
and had sex with that man.
The only difference between
Him and the street thug hotshot,
is that he got money
without the mug shot!
And mom, please forgive me for sayin
but I think you sold out,
for more than just the pipe he was layin
Aww momma, you know that I love you,
but I just gotta know
Did you forget that I'd need my daddy
When I started to grow?
Was the money worth it momma
'cause I still feel alone?
We got a house, but it don't feel like a home.
Momma stop cryin'
I just gotta say how I'm feelin'
With all these inner thoughts
my mind is racin' and reelin'
I know you love me.
I know it-I know it!
And everyday you try real hard to show it.
But I need a man to teach me how to be a man.
And-it's just that, well,
I'd rather have my daddy around to do it.
And my sister needs a father
So when these boys start to holler
She will have a protector
To keep her from bein' bothered.
Plus our community gonna always lack
If a daughter ain't got her dad

to watch after her back.
And momma I know you strong
and you doin' the best you can;
and you can teach me a lot of things,
but it was-*Never* God's plan
For a woman to teach
a man how to be a man.

The Park

sun kissed dew drops

plastic faces

lovers once loved

distinct places

children playing

football passes

untied laces

lads and lasses

rushing waters

courts cement brick

chocolate bars

soft blankets thick

fires blazing

hot barbecue

fathers saying

i sure love you

Death of an Empire

How is it that love dies?

Is it possible to know?

> On summer evenings
> while the warm wind blows
> love plays the puppets
> in the puppeteers show...

The regime reached a phenomenal peak,
but the empire expanded too far.
As with all empires
when the territory becomes too vast
the emperors lose control
and the empire falls apart.

Shattered foundations are the only remnants
of what once was.
So it happens with love.
When the regions that were once
easily conquered
become insurmountable.

Souls changing to meet the demands of life
Do not always adjust for the superior.

Love Scene

Al Jarreau said

that no matter come what may

love would prevail.

What about when it fails?

                    LOVE

Is not a storybook

of roses without thorns

and the heavens have not promised

only blue skies.

Can love fly on broken wings?

Or is the final answer that love dies?

The sun never rises

on the west side of the world;

sometimes the clouds swathe

the essence of the stars.

At times the fantasy we strive to reach

is much too far.

Can all flights of imagination be fulfilled?

Will every star caress its reverie?

As the moon serenades the lovers of the world;

Will your love always be a part of me?

Memories of You

I remember it well
The last piece of advice
I got from you.

You said to me daughter
the best way to get back
at your enemies
is to be successful.

You tried to tell me other
things but it was hard to
listen when in
hypocrisy spoken.

So I cling to those words.
Any positive memories
I have of you
are summed up
in that one
constructive sentence.

So I suppose something
is better
than nothing.

On the cusp of age 11

i read a speech that day
and i heard all the adults clap hard and loud
made me proud
my father says did you really write that
of course i said
wondering why he'd asked
didn't know what to think
just grabbed my gown
and roses from my mom
hugged her tight
and smiled
when she tucked me in that night

on the cusp of age 14
i sang a song
everyone clapped
soft and respectful
not like when i read the speech
still I felt elated
'cause i did it
on the ride home though
I was deflated
'cause my father says to me that it was awful you know
really bad really bad
and that made me feel bad
when I should have been feeling good
'cause i thought
wow you couldn't find one good thing to say
i had to have done something right
right?

so I just grabbed my gown
buried my face in it
held it tight
and cried
when momma
tucked me in that night

on the cusp of age 16
i stopped inviting you to things
since you'd already crushed
my singing dream
among other things
i sang in silence
while I played on my sports teams
praying you would not show up
to point out all my faults
I sure could hear you in my head though
wow, you got a lot of fouls
next time stay in the lane
don't you know what a three second zone is
those other girls sure are better than you

crossing the bridge
between 17 and 18
graduation
was supposed to be a beautiful thing
but you didn't even show up
didn't even let my little brother come
didn't even buy me
a graduation gift
couldn't you celebrate
one accomplishment
i mean
i was in the top 5%

In The Absence of My Father

at the starting gate of 24
college graduation
hmm, where have I seen this before
such a familiar door
still I wasn't prepared for
this repeat of history
probably just as well
'cause far as I could tell
i probably would've
done something wrong there too
just seemed like
there was never any pleasing you

still
despite my better judgment
i extending to you the olive branch
on my wedding day
i invited you to walk me down the aisle
almost wish I hadn't now
to be fair
you didn't say anything negative
but in the absence of a word positive
it might as well have been a negative
then I found out
the gift you gave
you didn't even pick it out
what the hell is that about
was I not worth a little thought

on to the cusp of 28 when you came to see
our new house
what a grouse
instead of telling me that you were proud

i had to hear you say aloud
i would never have bought this house
too much carpet
too many stairs
too much wallpaper on the wall
see
but here's what I don't recall
no one asked your opinion
at all

still
between that day
and our children births
you had moments of redemption
when I thought
maybe we could work our differences out
then
your step kids
started having
step-grandkids
and I started to see
history
replicating for me
familiar scenes
this surreal vista was being painted anew
and i since i don't like the view

i see on the cusp of 36
for my children's sake
i'm placing a new picture in front of their horizon
there will be no room for questioning
on the day they read their speeches
or negativity on the day
they sing their songs

In The Absence of My Father

on the sidelines
when they play their games
there will be no constant
pointing out of their wrongs
we will surround their lives
with seas of positive voices
create countermeasures
for the evil they will meet
as they walk through life there will be those
who will work diligently
to bust their pride
but the sin should never come from
those on the inside

On Sunday

my brother says to me
you are in all things far too emotional

how I ask
can the created thing be anything less
than what the Creator created it to be

my brother says to me
you are too bitter and negative

thus, i sigh
wondering
how much of me is God made
and how much of me is made
by the parents God gave me

i say to my brother
rather I respond to my brother

hmm
bitter
i guess i am
coffee in need of cream
nightmare in search of a daydream
dreaming of the day
when the sweet Lena of first grade
will return

i say to my brother
rather I ask of my brother

In The Absence of My Father

don't you ever get bitter
doesn't it bother you to be constantly replaced
if you say anything other than of course
you dear brother are a liar

What I Heard Was

I heard a woman say
"I didn't need a man!
"I didn't need a man to:
    "Help me raise my kids
        "Help me pay my bills
            "Help me do anything!
    "I didn't even need a man for sex!
    "I had plenty of toys for that."

I heard her son say
"She don't need me!
"She don't need me to
    "Help her raise my kids
        "Help her pay the bills
            "Help her do anything!
    "She don't even need me for sex.
    "She got plenty of toys for that."

My momma didn't have my daddy to help raise me and I turned out just fine.

I heard two women cry that day.

The Good Father

He is nobler than any human king
And serves for far more nobler reasons
His sacrifice serves as witness
Against those who commit fatherly treason

He serves:

For the sound his son makes
when he breathes in at night
for the smile of his daughter
when the sun cast its full light

for the look of the moon
as they chase fireflies
for the free wind at their feet
when they run fast with blue skies

for the sweet swish of sand
on a hot summer day
for the snowballs frigid cold
during a fun winter's play

for the joy they do bring him
with silly songs; weird dances
for the life they breathe in him
with their crazy ways; antics

for squealing wheels on pavement
when their bikes crash to the ground
for the thump in his chest
as he turns toward the sound

for the heartbeats he feels
when he holds them closely
for the love in their keen eyes
when he bandages skinned knees

for unreserved hugs
at the end of a hard day
for love unconditional
and for a reason to pray

The good father loves perfectly as God
Casting out fear

So for every father within the sound of my voice
For every father who made the elective choice
To man up and accept responsibility
Who anted up; operating unselfishly

I salute you today and forevermore
Knight you as you have never been before
A noble more brave than any rank at roundtable
Unwavering in commitment, steady, secure and stable

You true trench heroes paternal
Partakers of this ceremony informal
Who viewing words upon impersonal parchment
Deserve more than cursory acknowledgement

For you serve for far more nobler reasons than
        patriotism, revenge, or righteousness
You simply serve
Because you love
What could ever be more splendid than that?

On Stone Ground

Hatred spilled from my lips then
blood red
Vampire droplets
of bitterness and gall
I tried hard
to purge the venom from my system
Vomiting
acidic words on the page
till my rage was spent
Spewing
expressions of language so raw
finding pen and ink my astringent
Churning out
paper penned dissertations
till anger was no more
Emitting
light into places of darkness
Discovering a new and freeing door
Acceptance eaten slowly
found its way inside
Remedying fluttering viscera
Joyous laughter resounds

Father is still far away
Alas, my soft heart is found
Is no longer low-nor
broken on stone ground

no more excuses

up you slacker; 'wake
from your bed of affliction
no more excuses

up you sluggard; rise
from self-imposed addiction
end your defenses

cool waters of forgiveness
wash waves of life over your soul

forgiveness haiku

as aloe vera
on wounds are the words I'm sor-
ry to human hearts

father

factoring in my

assessment and

taking into account my life experiences I

have noted that they can be

effortlessly ir-

responsible

Father

Faithful in devotion
Accountable and
Trustworthy always
Helpful and
Endlessly
Reliable

The Finish

When your dreams have been broken in pieces
and your hopes appear as glass shattered.
Remember, it's not how you started,
it's how you finish that matters.

Though through the course of this life you may falter
and the end seems nowhere in sight.
Remember, the sun always arises,
to displace the dark of the night.

Through faith there are mountains to conquer
and yes valleys yet to go through.
Yet if we but trust in the Master
no dream is too lofty for our hearts to pursue.

Hope is contained in the spirit
that believes on broken wings it can still fly.
Towards the new life in tomorrow,
as it tosses today's torments aside.

In this life as we strive for perfection
some dreams may become broken and shattered.
Remember, it's not how you started,
it's how you finish that matters.

Lena Arnold is the author of *For This Child We Prayed: Living with the Secret Shame of Infertility, For This Dream We Prayed Companion Journal,* and *Strong Black Coffee: Poetry and Prose to Enlighten, Encourage, and Entertain Americans of African Descent.* Lena and her husband Horace started *IN*fertility Press, an imprint of Emperor Publishing, in an effort to dispel many of the myths associated with infertility in both the African-American and Christian communities.

Her work has been featured in numerous periodicals, and will soon be featured in *"Free to Fly: Transitions for the Seasons in a Woman's Life,"* published by InSCRIBEd Inspirations. As a motivational speaker, Lena applies the lessons learned from clinical infertility to the social, emotional and spiritual infertility many of us feel in various areas of our lives. As a wife, and mother of three—including her "double blessing" of twin sons—Lena seeks to encourage and empower women, men, and young people to "give birth" to all their dreams!

Lena is also a respected consultant on family and youth issues and has spent the last 20 years working tirelessly on their behalf. She is primarily responsible for helping non-profits & businesses achieve organizational goals through the creation of effective development strategies.

Lena attended Lincoln University in Missouri on a theater scholarship before returning home to Dayton, where she completed her degree in Communications from the Wright State University School of Liberal Arts. She began her career as a journalist and has written for several publications within the Dayton community where she currently resides.

Ever active in the arts community, she works with her husband's family company, **Arnold Signature Events**, to plan and implement the *Paul Laurence Dunbar Java, Jazz, and Poetry Series* to raise funds for local arts organizations, while at the same time encouraging and promoting new and emerging local talent.

Lena is also consistently sought out as a motivational speaker for her dynamic public speaking and theatrical abilities.

For more information, email lena@infertilitypress.com.

Books by Lena M. Fields-Arnold

Strong Black Coffee: Poetry and Prose to Encourage, Enlighten, and Entertain Americans of African Descent
Retail Price: $12.95
ISBN-13: 978-0979561337

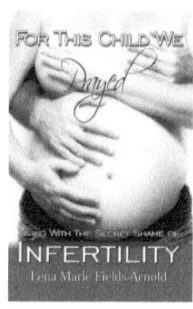

For This Child We Prayed: Living with the Secret Shame of Infertility
Retail Price: $14.95
ISBN Number: 978-0-9795613-0-6

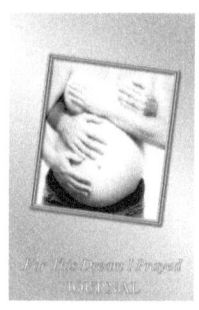

For This Dream I Prayed: Journal
Retail Price: $12.95
ISBN: 978-0979561313

www.ingramcontent.com/pod-product-compliance
Lightning Source LLC
Chambersburg PA
CBHW032017290426
44109CB00013B/691